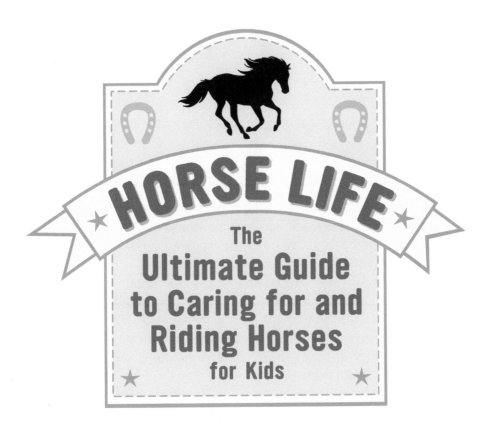

HORSE LIFE

The
Ultimate Guide
to Caring for and
Riding Horses
for Kids

Written by Robyn Smith
Illustrated by Kate Francis

ROCKRIDGE
PRESS

To God, for everything.

To my husband, Mark, for understanding.

To all the four-legged partners who have taught me more about humans and life than I could have possibly imagined. And especially to a horse named Robbin (no, I didn't name her). She was the heartbeat who started the human-training business with me. She taught me compassion, forgiveness, resilience, honesty, and, most importantly, a growing love for humans. For this I am eternally grateful.

Contents

Introduction

Have you always wanted a horse or pony? Do you have a horse and want to learn more? Well, this guide is for you.

This guide will help you grow as a new horse owner, someone who hopes to have a horse someday, or someone who just plain loves horses. We'll cover horse care, groundwork, riding, nutrition, breeds, and much more. Whether you ride for pleasure or competition, you'll find the information you need. By selecting a horse with the personality and age that suits you best, you'll be well on your way to success. More importantly, you'll learn that the relationship between a horse and a human is a journey worth taking.

My horse life began as a young child. I've been in love with horses from the age of three, according to my family. I even tried to ride our Great Dane once. At five years old, I visited my grandfather's nearby farm and realized that he had ponies.

After that day, my grandfather would often harness his team of Welsh ponies to a cart, and we would travel up and down the country roads while he taught me all about horses. Horses have been a part of my life ever since.

Although owning and caring for a horse has not always been easy or fun, the relationships I formed with horses helped me learn responsibility and improved my relationships with humans. I have rescued, retrained, and rehomed horses for more than 45 years. I have competed in competitive trail and endurance, and I've fallen in love with classical dressage. I now spend my days riding for pleasure and training humans about horses.

As you begin your journey with horses, remember that asking for help or advice is one of the most important ways to stay safe and learn. Ask someone who has grown up around horses or is an equine expert to teach you what you need to know. And remember, never stop learning.

Now open these pages and let's get your horse life started!

CHAPTER

1

Horse Life

Welcome to the amazing and wonderful world of horse life!

Have you wondered about horses' life cycles and when a horse can be trained and ridden for the first time? Did you know that horses use both their voices and a silent language to communicate with one another and with humans? Have you seen or experienced horse **behavior** you did not understand? Did you know that you can have a safe and fun relationship with a horse if you know when and whom to ask for help?

This chapter will cover these and other topics. You'll learn the horse's unique life cycle from happy **foal** to healthy senior citizen. Milestones along the way will teach you when you can train and ride a horse, how horses learn, and who should teach them. You'll learn how to recognize good behavior and when to report unacceptable behavior. We'll talk about how experts can help you succeed in building a relationship with horses.

The more knowledge you show about a horse's nature, the more willing a horse is to be your partner and cooperate. Let's get started!

From Foal to Full-Grown

In this section, we'll look at the unique life cycle of horses, from birth to senior citizen. Although it's exciting to raise a young horse, you should be careful and work with experts to keep you and your young horse safe.

11 Months/340 Days

On average, a pregnant **mare** carries one foal for 340 days (approximately 11 months). Occasionally, she will have twins.

One Day Old

Foals may be handled by people soon after they are born. They can be trained to wear a halter, learn to respect human space, and be led to and from the field. It's best to start training foals when they're small. Some **breeds** grow faster and taller than others and may become quite a handful later.

Four Months to One Year Old

By the time the curious, rapidly growing foal has reached four months, he's running, eating grass, and playing games with his mom or other foals in the field. At four to eight months, foals are weaned—they no longer rely on milk from their mothers for food. These foals are then called **weanlings**.

While a foal is still with his mother, he can learn how to get into and out of a trailer and how to let trainers groom and clip his coat.

Yearling

Foals are called **yearlings** from one year old until they are two. A yearling is ready for more advanced **groundwork**. Groundwork is training that gets the yearling ready for riding by building confidence and trust in humans.

Three Years Old

At three to four years old, many horses are trained to prepare for a rider. Some horses may mature more slowly and need to wait another year or so to be ridden. Training continues with more exposure to saddles and other equipment.

Four Years Old

Most four- to five-year-old horses have reached their full height and weight and are considered adults. Some breeds continue to grow in size and mature until the age of six. These are the prime years to learn and interact with humans in different environments.

Eight Years Old

Depending on the horse's personality, breed, training, and **type**, a horse of this age can be good for an advanced beginner. Typically, horses older than 10 years are suitable for beginners. More on finding your perfect horse in chapter 2.

Senior Citizen

With modern advances in nutrition and early management of age-related diseases, horses are enjoying healthy senior years well into their 20s and 30s.

Well-trained seniors are best for inexperienced riders and first-time horse owners, as well as for school or therapy horses. Senior horses tend to be calmer in a variety of environments. They usually cost less to buy, but they have so much to offer.

According to the *Guinness Book of World Records*, the longest-living horse was 62 years old! His name was Old Billy, and he lived in England from 1760 to 1822.

What's My Neighme?

Horses have unique names throughout their life cycle. The following terms will help you learn how to speak to horse people.

- **Broodmare:** female kept for having foals
- **Sire:** male parent of a foal
- **Dam:** female parent of a foal
- **Foal:** baby under one year old
- **Yearling:** foal between one and two years old
- **Weanling:** weaned foal
- **Filly:** female under three years old
- **Mare:** female over three years old
- **Colt:** male under three years old
- **Stallion:** male over three years old
- **Gelding:** castrated male
- **Pony:** a small type of horse
- **Breed:** a kind of horse

Horse Anatomy 101

When spending time around horses, you need to know some standard terms and locations of body parts. Riding instructors, **veterinarians**, and other **equestrians** use these terms when talking about injuries, grooming, and riding equipment. Take your time memorizing these parts, and you, too, will sound like an experienced horse person.

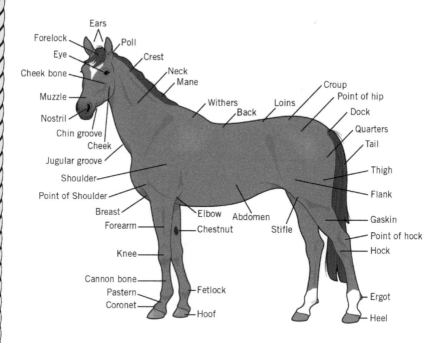

 Horses have the largest eyes of all land mammals. The placement of their eyes allows them to see most of their body and all around them.

You Herd Me

To understand horses, you must understand the world through their point of view. Horses are prey animals—other animals hunt them in the wild—and they naturally know how to signal to one another to flee from danger, especially from predators. As with other prey animals, safety is in numbers. The more eyes, ears, and noses to sense danger, the safer the **herd**.

Through highly tuned senses, distinctive body language, and vocalizations, the wild herd is prepared to escape danger. This alertness explains why some domestic horses are easily alarmed, spook quickly, and shy away from unfamiliar objects or sudden noises. Learning horse behavior and language will help you develop a safe and happy relationship with your horse.

Who's Who

Horse herds in the wild are mostly made up of young fillies and colts, one stallion, and many mares, one of which is the lead mare. Using her experience and natural leadership skills, the lead mare makes decisions that keep the herd safe. She leads them to grazing, water, and shelter, and away from known predator hideouts. Horses like to roam—this keeps their grazing areas fresh with new food and keeps predators busy looking for them.

The mares teach and train the colts and fillies in survival skills and acceptable behavior. When a young horse's behavior disrupts the balance in the herd, the stallion or mares drive the filly or colt away. The disruptive horse then joins another herd. When the young colts get older and challenge the stallion, he drives them from the herd. These male horses may form a bachelor herd without females. Every horse knows its position in the herd and carefully follows the rules of behavior.

The stallion has an important role. He is the father of the foals and the protector. He fights off other stallions from stealing the mares and defends the herd from predators.

 Feral horses are domestic horses that have escaped captivity and are mistakenly referred to as wild. Feral horses in the United States are called mustangs.

Horse Play

Most horses do not live in the wild now, but herd behavior is still part of their instincts, which is why play and bonding are so important. It's best for young horses to grow up with other horses. They play-fight, which decreases the risk of serious injuries when they are larger and stronger. The social skills learned through play are vital to a horse's overall well-being.

Horses IRL

Horses in the wild have developed certain traits or behaviors to survive. Their vision, smell, and hearing are highly tuned to detect danger. When horses sense danger, they lift their heads and freeze while they try to locate and identify the threat. Horses paw the ground to communicate, break up ice, enlarge water holes, and dig through the snow to find food in winter. Stallions posture and snort at rivals to show that they are the boss or want to be the boss of a **band** of mares. Stallion fighting is a common behavior, but it's rare for them to die from it.

Horses are born to learn. They mimic their mothers and other horses from birth. They also learn good and bad behavior from experience.

Horse Talk

Horses use body language and vocalizations with one another to express how they are feeling. A horse uses her ears, eyes, head, tail, and legs to signal to other horses. A horse can also squeal, snort, and whinny to express distress or pleasure. Understanding the different signals helps you know how your horse is feeling and what she's trying to communicate.

Horses often use warning signals before using physical contact, such as biting or kicking. When horses are mad, they threaten by pinning their ears back or turning their hind ends toward one another in warning.

Ears forward; head reaching toward you
She's saying hello or looking for treats.

Body tense; head and tail high
He may be ready to bolt.

Neck outstretched; teeth bared

She's warning she might bite.

Head up; ears forward; gaze fixed

He's trying to identify a distant object.

Lying down; eyes closed

She's sleeping.

Head high; curling upper lip

He's sniffing an unfamiliar smell.

Standing on back legs

She's rearing, which could be a sign of fear.

Pawing with front feet

He's bored, angry, or nervous.

Swishing tail; relaxed body
He's probably trying to keep flies away.

Back legs up; head down
She's bucking, which could be a sign of discomfort or fear.

Head outstretched; mouth open; eyes closed
She's yawning!

Reading a horse's body language takes practice. Ask a skilled horse person to help you understand your horse's behavior.

CHAPTER

2

The Perfect Horse— For You!

Horses come in a variety of shapes, colors, and sizes. Choosing, leasing, or purchasing the right horse is exciting and requires knowledge and expertise. Color or breed doesn't matter as much as matching you with the horse's type, size, **temperament**, experience level, and training for the activity you plan to do.

In this chapter, you'll learn about the types and breeds of horses, as well as the jobs they can do, which will help you understand more about them. Later in this chapter, you can decide what horse would be best for you. Not ready to own a horse yet? That's okay. You have plenty of time to learn and dream of a horse of your own someday.

Just My Type

The classification of horses can be confusing. For this guide, the horses are organized into five types. For each type, we'll look at typical breeds and activities that type of horse was bred to do. Although there are generally only three types of horses, I added gaited horses and ponies so you could better understand their unique **characteristics**.

Keep in mind, there are **crossbred** or mixed-breed horses that often have the best of both types of breeds. Just like us, horses are individuals. A horse may not always fit the description of its type.

Give Me a Hand

Horse height is measured in "hands." One hand is equal to four inches. Locate a horse's withers—the highest point on a horse's back—and measure from the ground to this point. Next, take the total inches and divide it by four. On average, horses are 14.2 hands and taller, and ponies are under 14.2 hands.

Type 1: Draft Horses or Cold-Bloods

Draft horses are typically tall, heavyweight horses bred for strength, size, and ability to pull heavy loads. They can grow to over 18 hands. These horses are often called "cold-blooded" because of their calm and easygoing temperament and the chilly northern regions where they first came from. Draft horses aren't fast, but they are strong and gentle. They compete in harness races, pull wagons and carriages, and are becoming more popular as riding horses. Common breeds include the Belgian, Percheron, Clydesdale, and Friesian.

Some breeds are called "light draft horses," like the Norwegian Fjord. These horses are smaller and sometimes called "ponies" due to their size, stocky build, and resistance to cold. Fjords are versatile and can compete in many sports. They make great riding horses—also known as mounts—for younger or small riders.

Type 2: Light Horses or Hot-Bloods

Light horses, often called "hot-bloods," are horses bred for speed, agility, and endurance (ability to travel long distances). These horses first came from warmer climates. They come in all sizes and shapes. Light horses are leaner-muscled, quick, and sensitive, and tend to have a let's-go attitude. Experienced riders who like speed are better suited to this type of horse.

Light horses are used in many jobs and sports such as hunter-jumping, racing, ranch, and stock work. Common breeds include the Arabian, Thoroughbred, American Quarter Horse, Paint Horse, Saddlebred, Standardbred, Tennessee Walking Horse, and Morgan.

A stock horse is a small, agile kind of horse that works well with livestock, especially cattle. The American Quarter Horse and Paint Horse are typical examples.

Type 3: Warmbloods

Warmbloods are a middleweight type of horse. They are the result of generations of crossbreeding the easygoing draft horse with the quick and agile light horse. Warmbloods come in a variety of sizes, shapes, and colors. They are popular in today's competitive show world and excel in many sports such as dressage, show jumping, three-day eventing, and harness sports. They are often seen in Olympic equestrian events. Common breeds include Hanoverians, Dutch and Swedish Warmbloods, and Trakehners.

Type 4: Gaited Horses

Gaited horses are considered light horses, bred for riding with smooth **gaits**. Historically, these horses were bred for wealthy landowners. Today's gaited horses typically excel at trail riding and showing. Common breeds include the Icelandic, Peruvian Paso, American Saddlebred, Tennessee Walking Horse, and Rocky Mountain Horse.

Type 5: Ponies

Ponies are considered horses and are commonly defined by their size, stocky build, thick coats, and tolerance to cold weather. They are under 14.2 hands, strong, versatile, and quick learners. Due to their size, small adults and children find them to be just the right size to compete or ride for fun. Ponies excel in many sports, but some shows are made for only ponies. Common breeds include the Icelandic, Shetland, Fell Pony, Welsh Mountain Pony, and Connemara.

 Miniature horses are not considered ponies. They are bred to resemble a full-size horse on a smaller scale—a much smaller scale. To be registered, they must be under 34 inches tall at the withers.

A Breed of Their Own

Some research claims there are more than 250 breeds of horses. A breed is a type of animal developed for a particular purpose or quality. In this section, we will cover some of the popular breeds.

American Quarter Horse

This popular, versatile, short, stocky breed has excellent muscle development for short distance sprinting, barrel racing, and all kinds of cattle work.

American Paint Horse

With broad, colorful spotting patterns of white and dark hair, American Paint Horses are of Western stock and are commonly used in Western pleasure riding and reining.

Appaloosa

Recognized by their colorful coat patterns, Appaloosas are prized for their versatility and easygoing disposition. They are found in a variety of sports and pleasure settings.

Arabian

Identified by its finely chiseled head, dished (indented) face, high tail carriage, and long, arching neck, this type of horse is versatile in the show ring and excellent on trails.

Morgan Horse

Morgan horses are compact, muscular, and refined. They support many interests, from pleasure riding to competitive sporting disciplines.

Thoroughbred

Known for speed and spirit, Thoroughbreds are tall, slim, and athletic. They are used for racing, jumping, and other speed sports.

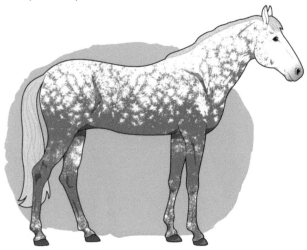

American Saddlebred

This popular gaited breed excels in the show ring, but its gentle temperament makes it an exceptional pleasure horse.

Standardbred

Built like a Thoroughbred, this type of horse can be 14 to 17 hands high. Standardbreds are best known for their ability in harness racing.

Tennessee Walking Horse

Tennessee Walking Horses generally range in height from 14.3 to 17 hands. This breed is recognized as an excellent trail, show, and pleasure mount.

Clydesdale

This draft horse stands 17 to 18 hands tall and has silky leg feathers. Historically used for farming, Clydesdales are gaining popularity for pleasure riding and showing.

Friesian

Typically black and powerfully muscled, this draft breed has a long mane, tail, and leg feathers. Friesians are popular in the show ring and for pulling carriages.

Norwegian Fjord

This durable and ancient breed is known for its exceptionally gentle temperament. This horse's small stature makes it an excellent starter horse for small people.

Pony of the Americas

At 11.2 to 13 hands high, this small, colorful breed helps smaller riders of all ages gain confidence in the show ring, on trails, and in many sports.

Shetland Pony

In certain shows, this breed should not exceed 11.5 hands (46 inches). When trained properly, these tough and sturdy ponies are the perfect starter horses for children due to their size and temperament.

Miniature Horse

This breed doesn't exceed 34 inches but isn't considered a pony. Although miniature horses appear in the show ring, they are often used as companions or therapy animals.

 Przewalski's horse, originally from Mongolia, is believed to be the only truly wild horse species still in existence.

Color Coated

Horses come in a variety of colors and patterns. The first four in the following list are the base colors that combine to form all other colors. The term "black points" means a black mane, tail, and legs.

Bay

Reddish brown, or dark brown with black points.

Black

Solid black coat.

Brown

Coat color can be different shades of brown.

Chestnut

Light to dark red coat without black points.

Sorrel

Light reddish or yellow coat, sometimes with a blond mane and tail.

Palomino

Golden coat with a white mane and tail.

Buckskin

Yellowish-gray coat with dark points, often mistaken for dun.

Dun

Gray-gold or tan, with a sandy yellow to a reddish-brown body color that typically has a stripe down the back and/or legs and neck.

Gray

Coat can be light to very dark with black-and-white hairs on black skin.

Appaloosa

A coat color that comes in a variety of spotted patterns.

On Your Mark!

Horses have distinctive body markings that help us identify them. Here are some common examples found on their heads and legs.

Head Markings

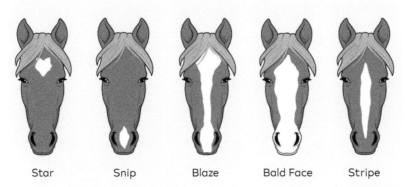

| Star | Snip | Blaze | Bald Face | Stripe |

Leg Markings

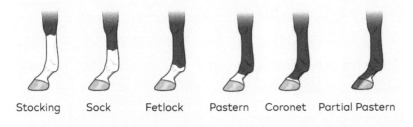

| Stocking | Sock | Fetlock | Pastern | Coronet | Partial Pastern |

Hoof colors vary from blue-black or black to white and may have dark stripes.

Choosing a Horse

Now that you've learned about the types and breeds of horses and the jobs they can do, what else do you need to know?

Choosing a horse successfully comes down to one important rule: Always ask for professional help from your riding instructor, a local veterinarian, and/or another equestrian expert. Here are some of the traits they'll help you consider.

Temperament

Temperament is a horse's disposition, nature, character, and personality. Beginners should choose a calm, easygoing horse.

Training Level

Have a riding instructor assess your riding skill and match you with a horse's training level. Being matched with the horse that's right for you is important for your safety and long-term success.

Health and Soundness

Your vet will look for signs of health and soundness during the horse's exam. Soundness is a lack of lameness and illness in a horse.

Conformation and Movement

Conformation is the overall correctness of a horse's body proportions. Undesirable conformation can affect the horse's movement, which could limit his ability to perform a specific task.

Size

When selecting the size of your horse, consider your height and expected growth, the activity you want to do, and your body build.

Age and Sex

Whether you choose a mare or a gelding, it's always wise to choose an older, more experienced horse for a beginner and leave the young, speedy mounts for the experienced equestrians.

CHAPTER

3

Ready to Ride

Now that you've chosen the perfect horse, the next step is preparing to ride. Building a partnership with your horse is one of life's greatest pleasures.

For horse lovers everywhere, there's nothing more exciting than imagining yourself on the back of your own horse. She's beautiful, fast, and athletic. Her mane is flowing, her ears are forward, and she's ready to gallop, jump over logs, and take you wherever you want to go. Sounds amazing, right? Before you ride, there are a few important things you need to know to keep you and your horse safe.

Whether you're already taking lessons or hope to in the future, this chapter will help you prepare. You'll learn what gear you'll need and the names of the four movements horses do while in motion. Let's gear up!

Horse Gear

Horse gear is commonly referred to as "tack" and "equipment." How you ride—Western or English style—will affect the gear you'll need to ride your horse. English-style riding uses more direct pressure for communicating with the horse through the seat, legs, and hands. Western-style riding uses more indirect pressure. Keep in mind that the fit of the gear is very important. If your horse is in pain or discomfort, she may not behave like you want her to.

Ask an expert for help in selecting the correct gear that not only fits you and your horse properly but is appropriate for the style you wish to ride. Check your tack regularly for safety, neatness, cleanliness, adjustment, and condition. Replace damaged tack if it can no longer be safely repaired.

Halter

The halter is the basic tool for leading your horse. Halters can be made of leather, nylon, or rope. There are special safety halters designed for horses that panic and pull back when tied. The halter is placed on your horse's head with a rope attached.

Lead Rope

Lead ropes are attached to the halter by a snap. They come in different lengths, thicknesses, and materials. Like the halter, the lead rope needs to be in good condition. It should be free from knots, frayed ends, and damaged snaps.

Bit

Bits are made of metal or rubber and are placed in the horse's mouth. They communicate to your horse through direct or indirect pressure. The most common bit, used by both Western and English riders, is the single-joint snaffle (left). Western riders also use a curb bit (right).

Hackamore

Hackamores are used in place of a bridle and bit. Popular with both English and Western riders, hackamores apply pressure across the nose instead of in the mouth. The main difference between the English (left) and Western (right) style is the length of the shanks—the metal bars that hang down on both sides of the hackamore. Western shanks are longer.

Bridle

The bit and reins attach to a bridle. The bridle is slipped over the horse's head and around his ears, and the bit is gently placed inside his mouth. English (left) and Western (right) riders use distinct styles of bridles, each with additional parts attached.

Reins

Reins attach to each side of the bit or hackamore. They are an **aid** to the hands in communicating directly to your horse. Reins can be split, separate, or connected by a buckle depending on the riding style.

Boots

Boots protect the horse's legs while he performs certain tasks. Boots come in different sizes and shapes and are specific to the activity that exposes the horse's legs to injury. They are worn on the front, back, or all four legs. Bell boots (left) and splint boots (right) are two common types of boots.

 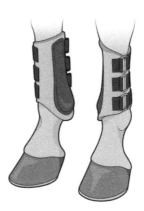

Saddle

Saddles were designed for specialized jobs. They have stirrups for your feet and require a saddle pad or blanket to be comfortable for your horse. English saddles (top) were designed to carry riders over flat or uneven ground and jumps. Western saddles (bottom) were designed for working livestock. They have a part called a "horn" that is useful for riders who take care of cattle.

Breast Collar

A breast collar prevents the saddle from slipping when the horse is going uphill or jumping. The Y-shaped collar attaches to the saddle on either side of the horse's neck and at the saddle's girth or cinch. The cinch is attached to both sides of the saddle, which allows it to hold the saddle in place around the horse's body behind her front legs. Western collars are typically thicker and heavier than English ones.

 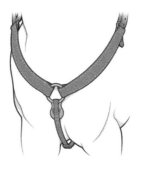

 Riders use aids to communicate with their horse. Natural aids are the seat, legs, and hands. Whips and spurs, when used properly, assist the natural aids.

Human Gear

Like horses, humans need the right gear. Whether you are mucking stalls, pleasure riding, competing, or just hanging out at the barn, selecting the right gear keeps you safe.

Helmet

Wearing a properly fitted horse-riding helmet with the ASTM/SEI (American Society for Testing and Materials/Safety Equipment Institute) seal is the safest practice around horses. Your most vulnerable body part is your head. A horse can swing its huge head into yours while turning or lifting it to look at something.

Boots

English-style riding boots fit to the knee, and paddock boots fit above the ankle. Western-style boots fit between the ankle and knee. Both styles come in a variety of shapes, sizes, and colors. The heels are at least one inch high to prevent your foot from being caught in a stirrup.

China is credited with inventing the first stirrup around 100 CE. It was designed to support the foot while riding, creating more stability for the rider.

Spurs

Spurs are metal tools worn on the heels of riding boots to direct a horse. It's important to learn from a riding instructor how to use spurs properly. Spurs are not necessary for all riding activities.

Pants

English-style riding pants are called breeches or jodhpurs. They are snug-fitting and stretch to move with your leg. Western-style riders wear jeans that are designed for riding horses, and the legging covers the Western boot. It's important the pants fit properly.

Chaps

Chaps are worn over boots and pants to protect the rider and the gear from wear and tear. English-style half-chaps fit below the knee and are worn with shorter paddock boots. **Farriers**—horseshoeing professionals—and cowboys wear larger chaps to protect their legs when working with horses and livestock.

So Stylish!

English and Western riding styles differ in clothing and gear. For example, the English saddle is lighter and has a girth to keep the saddle secured to the horse. The Western saddle is heavier and has a cinch. English riders typically wear breeches, and Western riders wear jeans.

Gloves

Gloves protect your hands when riding and handling ropes or horses. Thicker gloves are worn when using farm tools to clean stables, repair fences, or remove brush or wire from fields. They are made of leather or sturdy material that resists tears.

Vest

Safety vests are worn during riding activities that require an added layer of chest and rib protection. The vest is worn over the shirt and secured to the body. High-impact sports such as jumping, rodeo, and endurance riding are a few activities that you'll need a vest for.

Shirt

Shirts should have at least short sleeves to protect the upper arm. They should be long enough to tuck into the waistband and be made of material that is comfortable and suitable for the weather. It's best to wear long sleeves to protect your arms when working on ranches and farms.

In January 2019, the United States Pony Club updated its rules to require that riders wear protective vests while riding in cross-country events.

Open the Gaits

A gait is a way to move on foot. Most horses move in four common gaits. Each gait has several **beats**—regularly timed movements—and may or may not involve suspension, which is a pause when all four limbs are off the ground.

It's important to understand the gaits to understand transitions. A transition is when you cue the horse to move from one gait into another. It takes practice for both you and your horse to become skilled at transitioning.

Walk

The walk is the foundation of the gaits and the slowest one. Each leg lifts separately during the completion of the stride. The walk has four beats and no moment of suspension.

Trot

The trot is a two-beat gait with diagonal pairs of legs moving together with a moment of suspension. The trot can be ridden while sitting or posting. Posting is when the rider moves up and down from the stirrups in rhythm with each diagonal pair of legs.

Canter

The canter (English) or lope (Western) is a three-beat gait with a moment of suspension and is faster than the trot. The canter has one front leg that **leads** by reaching out farther than the other leg.

Gallop

The gallop or run is the horse's fastest gait. It is a four-beat gait with suspension. Like the canter, the gallop has a lead.

Horses are unique among animals because they have many gaits.

CHAPTER

4

Safety Skills

When you're around horses, safety is the most important thing. Horses are large, powerful animals with quick reactions, and they're likely to run from danger. If your horse reacts quickly, you could become unbalanced and fall, and the horse could run off. You could be injured by being stepped on or knocked over. All horses are potentially dangerous, especially in an unfamiliar environment with new objects, other horses, and noise.

Loose horses pose a major safety hazard to themselves and others, especially when they are in an unfamiliar area without a fence, like a horse show or on the trails. It is important to practice safety skills with experts in a safe learning environment. The more experience you have with supervised instruction, the safer you will be when you are away from the stables.

This chapter will cover the safety skills you need to learn and practice. Following these tips will reduce the risk of injury to yourself, your horse, and others. Although most horses are gentle and are used to being handled, it's always wise to ask for help from experienced equestrians as you learn. The best way you can earn your horse's trust is to keep both of you safe.

Safe Spaces

Whether you're riding or doing groundwork, following these tips will keep you and your horse safe for many rides to come.

Give Your Horse Enough Space

The space where you tie your horse to be groomed, shoed, or bathed must be large enough for your horse to turn around and lift his head without touching low-hanging objects or ceilings. The space also needs to be clean and free from objects near the horse's legs. The ground should be level with packed dirt or a concrete floor with a rubber mat on top.

Use Crossties for Bathing

The bathing space must have a safe tying post or crossties. Crossties are long ties that attach to each side of the halter and then to the wall. Special clips or snaps should be used to prevent pullback injuries. The bathing supplies should be on shelves or in bins and out of the way.

Use a Breakaway Halter

Crossties are used in stable aisles between the stalls to groom and tack your horse. Use extreme caution and ask for help until you feel safe when using these ties. It is safer to use a special halter called a "breakaway." This halter is designed to break if a horse panics and pulls back suddenly.

Check Your Workspace

The arena or small corral where you ride or work your horse should be inspected for protruding objects, such as nails, hooks, wires, broken boards, and sharp metal pieces. The bridle and tack hooks should be away from any area where you tie your horse. Halters, bridles, and stirrups can easily become hooked.

Close the Gates

When working or riding your horse outside, make sure any gates that lead to the road are closed. Closing the gates is especially important while you are getting to know your horse. The pathways should be clear of debris and farm tools, and equipment should be stored away from riding areas.

 The term "horse sense" comes from Europe and originally meant an unsophisticated, country type of sense. Now, it means plain old common sense.

Safe Handling

Safe handling means using the safest methods when touching your horse when you groom, bathe, halter, lead, and ride. By practicing the following skills, you can prevent accidents and injuries.

Learn as Much as You Can

Before handling a horse, it is important to have knowledge, understanding, and experienced help. The horse should be calm and well-trained, and have an easygoing temperament. The best way to learn is by taking riding lessons, volunteering at a local stable, and learning from a skilled horse person.

Check Your Gear

Your horse and gear should be in good condition and suitable for your specific activity. Checking your gear before using it decreases the risk of equipment failure and injuries. The halter, lead rope, and snap are the primary gear you will need to handle your horse. Ask for help if you believe a piece of equipment is unsafe.

Catch Your Horse Safely

When approaching a horse in the field or paddock, make sure the horse sees and hears you so you don't startle him. Approach with your halter and lead rope ready from an angle, extending the halter and rope toward the horse in a friendly manner. Slip the rope around the horse's neck, then slip on the halter.

Make Sure Your Horse Sees You

Approach a tied horse at an angle toward her head while speaking to let her know you are there. Extend your hand and make sure the horse sees you before proceeding. Repeat this step each time you move away to change brushes or get gear. Never approach a horse from behind!

Keep Yourself Safe

When walking around a tied horse, walk out of kicking range or stay close with your hand on the horse's body and your belly button facing away. When grooming, keep your feet slightly apart for balance and stand parallel to the horse. This position will keep the horse from accidentally stepping on your toes.

Use Caution around the Head

Be very careful when handling a horse's face and head. While grooming the horse, keep your head off to one side and not directly over your horse's head. As cute and soft as a horse's nose seems, be careful when handling his nose and mouth. The horse cannot see what you are doing and may mistake your finger for a treat.

Blind Spots

Horses have blind spots where they can't see you. Keep these spots in mind when approaching or handling any horse:

- Directly behind the tail
- On the back behind the head
- In front of the forehead
- Under the head on the ground and near the front legs

Safe Riding

Knowing and practicing safe riding skills helps you, your horse, and others stay safe. Most accidents and injuries are preventable and result from a lack of knowledge. Follow these tips to stay safe.

Wear a Helmet

Wear a protective helmet when you're around horses. The helmet should be specifically designed for equestrians and in the style that suits your activity. If you take a tumble off a horse, most helmet manufacturers recommend you purchase a new helmet, which is the best practice.

Mount Up

Mount your horse in an area free from low overheads, lights, or objects protruding from the walls. If possible, use a mounting block. Make sure the block is on even, solid ground and does not move when you climb the steps. Face the same direction as your horse and mount up.

Check Riding Space

Get to know your horse in an enclosed area, such as a round corral or arena, for several rides before adventuring outside. Before climbing aboard your horse, walk her around the area unmounted. The riding area should be clear of objects that could frighten your horse as you are getting to know each other.

Take Riding Lessons

Sign up for riding lessons on your horse or a school horse. You'll learn how to handle unusual situations and how to recognize and prevent potentially dangerous situations. The instructor will help match you to a horse.

Ride with Others

When you're not taking lessons, ride with another rider or in a group, and always let someone know when and where you are riding. Horses like being with other horses until they have learned to trust you as the herd leader. They instinctively know that safety is in numbers.

 A "spook" or "shy" is when a horse makes a startled jump sideways or a quick change of direction with the intention to flee. It's usually caused by an unexpected or unfamiliar noise or object.

Rope Basics

Learning rope basics is important for tying and leading your horse. Use the following rope guidelines to keep you and your horse safe.

Tie Your Horse Safely

Tie your horse to a solid wall, post, or pole that does not move. The tying ring must be set deep within the wall or post to prevent it from falling out. Never tie your horse by the reins. Tying your horse by the reins could injure your horse's mouth if he becomes frightened and pulls back.

Use the Quick-Release Knot

This knot can easily release when you pull on the short end that is not attached to your horse. A quick-release knot will protect your horse from injuring her head and neck with the halter in the event that she becomes frightened and pulls back (see page 55).

Prepare to Lead

Standing at your horse's left shoulder and facing forward, hold the end of the lead rope in your left hand. Fold the extra rope. Hold the rope in the middle of the folds—never hold it looped around your hand. Your right hand holds the lead rope beneath the snap that is attached to the lead rope.

Lead Your Horse

Keeping your head up and eyes forward, focus on where you are going. Begin to walk, keeping your horse's shoulder next to you. Teach your horse to walk next to you and not ahead or behind, pulling on you. Ask for help until you have learned this important task.

Stop and Back Up

Ask your instructor to show you the different ways to have your horse halt, back up, and trot nicely next to you. It is important to practice these skills with help until you and your horse are performing these tasks safely.

Knot Me

This quick-release knot is one safe way to tie your horse.

1. Wrap the working end (not connected to the horse) through a ring or around a pole.
2. Leave enough rope on the end to pull under the looped end like a figure eight.
3. Fold the working end back under the post wrap, leaving a loop.

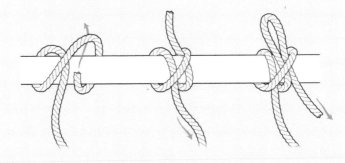

CHAPTER

5

Eating Like a Horse

Owning and caring for your own horse sounds exciting, but there are important things to learn and consider before making this big decision and commitment. Domestic horses depend on humans to care for them and keep them healthy and happy. It's wise to know all about caring for a horse before you own one.

In the following chapters, you will learn about taking care of your horse. Whether you plan on keeping your horse at home or at another place, you will need to know what to feed him and what to look for in a place to live. You'll also learn routine horse management, including grooming, bathing, health care, and more.

In this chapter, you'll learn about your horse's diet—the most important part of caring for your horse. The basic elements of a horse's diet are water, hay, grain, and minerals. Let's learn more!

Water

Horses need constant access to fresh, clean water. The average 1,000-pound horse drinks 10 to 15 gallons of water every day. They drink more during warm weather and less during cold. If you live in a colder winter climate, you'll need to either break up ice or put a special heater in the water to keep it from freezing.

Horses that live in a pasture can have access to fresh running water in a stream or river, but you'll have to make sure the source isn't polluted and doesn't dry up or freeze over for any part of the year.

Water can also be kept in containers, such as tubs or troughs, in the pasture. Containers come in many shapes, sizes, and human-made materials. The container should be large enough to provide each horse with a minimum of 10 to 15 gallons per day for no more than a week. These containers should be emptied out and cleaned at least every week to prevent algae from growing and mosquitoes from laying eggs in the water.

Smaller areas for horses, such as stalls or paddocks, may have smaller water containers that are easy to dump, refill, and move around. Horses should not be able to knock over the containers easily. Smaller containers need to be filled and cleaned more often than large ones do.

Horses that are hot, sweaty, and working—when they are trail riding or packing, for instance—can stop and drink along the way.

Hay

Horses are grazers and herbivores—they move around while nibbling plants, grass, and herbs for up to 20 hours a day. They need to consume large amounts of grass to create the fuel they need to stay at a healthy weight.

Grass is the horse's main source of food. It provides the roughage, or fiber, a horse needs for her gut to digest properly. When horses live in smaller spaces called paddocks, they need roughage in the form of hay. Hay is dried grass that has been grown in large fields, cut or mowed, and bundled into large wheels or blocks called bales. Hay and grass together are referred to as "forage."

Seed hay is quality grass called "rye" or "timothy." It's highly nutritious and best for hardworking horses. Meadow hay is softer and greener and made from many different plants. It is best for lightly worked horses.

Forage—grass and hay—makes up 50 to 100 percent of a horse's diet. It is the most important part of the horse's feed.

How Much?

In general, a full-grown horse needs about 15 to 30 pounds of hay per day. That is 1.5 to 3 percent of his body weight if he weighs 1,000 pounds. Some horses need more and some need less, depending on the horse's size, metabolism, and workload, the time of year, and whether the horse gets additional feed. Ask your vet for advice.

Feeders

It's best for hay to be fed throughout the day in bins or nets called "slow feeders." Horses can be fed from heavy bins on the ground or from a hay rack you can attach to a wall. Hay racks or nets should be attached securely and high enough that your horse won't catch his foot in it.

Grain

Horses often eat **cereal grains** like corn, oats, and barley. Sometimes they are fed only one type of grain, like oats, and sometimes they're fed a mixture. Ask your vet to help you choose the right grain.

Performance horses need more energy to jump, race, run long distances, and train. They need concentrated feed—also called mixed grains—to work and sustain a healthy weight. These horses simply cannot eat enough forage to meet the daily requirements for the additional work.

If a horse needs more protein for muscle mass development, he is in light-duty work, or he's prone to weight gain, he might need an additive called a "balancer." When you feed horses grain for energy, be sure to feed in smaller meals to decrease the volume of each meal.

How Much

The amount and type of grain to feed your horse depends on many factors—how much you work him, his age, and his weight. Overfeeding is a common problem and poses health risks for your horse. Your vet can help you choose any additional feed your horse may need in addition to his high-quality forage.

Grain Feeders

Grain feeders are containers that come in various shapes and sizes. They are mounted or securely hooked on walls at the level of the horse's head. Ground containers need to be made of rubber or other material that cannot get damaged or injure the horse if she steps in it.

Hay There!

Hay should be stacked and stored in a dry, enclosed area on top of pallets with good air circulation around the bales to prevent mold from spoiling the hay. Grain-type feed should be stored in tightly sealed, rodent-proof containers in a clean, organized feed room. Salt blocks can be stored on dry shelves.

Vitamins and Minerals

Salt Blocks

Horses need about one to two ounces of salt per day. Livestock salt blocks are convenient. They come in small or large sizes and can be used indoors or outdoors. The blocks are rougher on horse tongues than on cattle tongues, so many owners choose loose salt or horse licks instead.

Protein Blocks

Protein is the **nutrient** required for building muscle mass. When grass does not provide enough protein for a balanced diet, protein blocks can help. These blocks often have added vitamins and minerals, too.

Trace Minerals

Trace minerals and vitamins are small essential nutrients that help the horse's body stay happy and healthy. They are needed for proper nutrition and come loose or in premixed feed. It's best to ask your veterinarian for advice. Some vitamins and minerals can become harmful when a horse has too much.

High-fat feeds, oils, and rice bran are excellent sources of energy for performance horses. Fat is a more sustainable fuel than cereal grains alone.

Food Rules

Start with Basic Feed

Always start with fresh water, quality forage, and salt. Forage can be tested for vitamins and minerals. If it lacks any, you can add supplements to the horse's feed. Before adding cereal grains or protein balancers, talk to an expert. It's easy to add too many supplements and potentially harm your horse.

Use High-Quality Hay

Buy the best hay available in your area and have it tested for nutrients. Hay makes up 50 to 100 percent of your horse's diet. The better the hay, the less likely it is that your horse will need supplements.

Measure Your Hay

Start with the average formula of 15 to 20 pounds of hay per day for a 1,000-pound horse. Ask an expert to help you determine the weight of your horse and adjust the feed accordingly. Feed this amount for three to four weeks and watch your horse's weight. Adjust the hay as needed to maintain his healthy weight.

Use a Scale

To use a human standing scale, weigh yourself first, then have someone zero out the scale while you stand on it. Then, while still on the scale, hold a flake (a portion of hay). Add or remove hay until you have the exact weight to feed your horse.

Measure Your Grain

Place a measuring container on a scale and zero out the scale. Add the grain into the container until it reaches the recommended weight for your horse. Then find a container that fits the grain amount exactly. Now you have an accurate amount of feed without having to weigh each time.

Make Gradual Feed Changes

Make feed changes gradually over at least a week. Sudden changes in your horse's diet may cause gut problems that need to be treated by a vet. This principle applies to changing forage, grains, and supplements. Always add new feed items one at a time so you can know what has caused any unwanted effects.

Ask for Help

Learn from an expert how to determine the amount of forage your horse needs and whether she needs different types of added feeds. Observe and report changes in your horse's appetite, activity level, and weight, and learn how to adjust the feed.

Use Clean Containers

Clean your horse's feed and water containers regularly. Remove uneaten hay and inspect it for mold, inedible stems, and debris. If there is consistently leftover hay, try cutting back. If your horse seems hungry after eating, consider increasing the amount of hay.

Have a Regular Schedule

Like humans, horses like routines. Some may become so used to certain feeding times that they can become anxious and destructive when feed is late or inconsistent. Banging on doors, kicking walls, and weaving back and forth in the stall can be harmful to the horse and the stables.

Use Caution with Grass

Check with an expert before providing pasture access to your pony or horse. Grass varies from region to region and can contain high amounts of sugar at different growing periods during the year. Some breeds are more prone to health problems from eating grass.

Hand Graze

Horses are happiest when they're roaming and grazing. However, many horses do not have access to pastures, and others may not be able to eat much grass. Hand grazing your horse—walking her around the property with a lead rope while she grazes—will give you both satisfaction while spending time together.

CHAPTER

6

Stable Life

Just like you, horses need a safe place to live. They need shelter from weather, such as wind, rain, snow, and heat. They need a large space that is enclosed and free from dangerous objects that could injure them. Horses also need attention and care every single day.

Whether you keep your horse at home or board her at another location, you must know what to look for and what your horse needs to stay healthy and happy.

Before buying your perfect horse, you should know your budget, the type of horse, and the activity you plan to do. Your budget will help determine where your horse stays. Places range from reasonably priced self-care pastures with shelters to expensive full-care stables with daily paddock or pasture turnout.

Your activity will also help you choose where to keep your horse. If you plan to take lessons at a riding stable, you'll need your horse close by. If you plan to show and need the guidance of a horse trainer and riding instructor, you may need to board your horse at a stable that teaches your sport or activity.

In this chapter, we'll cover a variety of horse homes and discuss the advantages and disadvantages of each.

Pasture Perfect

For this guide, we will define a pasture as a large field with the purpose of growing grass for horses to graze. A pasture is the best environment for a domestic horse to roam, graze, and exercise, as long as you know the conditions that keep your horse healthy, safe, and secure.

Pastures

Many horse experts agree that one horse on at least one acre of well-managed grass is the best way to provide enough food for the horse. The land should be mostly flat, managed in a way to promote healthy seasonal growth, and free from poisonous plants and trees.

Some property owners have extra areas for horses to stay in temporarily so the pasture can rest and grow. This area may be another pasture or smaller areas called "dry lots" or "paddocks." In many regions, snow, ice, and other weather elements prevent year-round grazing. If that's the case where you live, you'll need to feed your horse hay when he's not able to graze.

One advantage for horse owners who own property is the lower cost. Buying feed and caring for your horse yourself is less expensive than paying someone else to do it. Other advantages include accurate feeding and being able to monitor the horse's appetite and check the horse for injuries and illnesses on a regular basis.

A pasture that is nearby and meets your needs could also be cost-effective. You could care for your horse yourself or pay a little more for someone else to feed him and keep an eye on him. Keeping your horse at another location is referred to as "boarding" your horse.

There are some disadvantages to pasturing your horse. If your horse lives in a pasture at home, the biggest disadvantage is manure management. Manure piles up fast. It attracts flies and needs to be picked up at least every week. You'll need a plan to handle the volume of manure your horse will create.

Another disadvantage is location. Horse owners who own property or pasture-board their horses need a truck and trailer to transport their horses to riding lessons, trail riding, or other activities.

Shelter

Shelters should be well-built, sturdy, and large enough to protect your horse in bad weather. You can have someone build the shelter, or you can buy it premade in different sizes, materials, and shapes. Inspect the shelter for loose or protruding nails, hooks, and wires. Horses like to chew on wood, so check the shelter frequently for chewed boards or posts that need replacing. Ask an expert how to keep your horse from chewing on the wood.

Fences and Gates

Fences and gates must be sturdy, secure, and free from sharp edges. Horses like to roam and will find gaps to go through and wood posts to chew on. Frequent inspections are important to avoid mishaps. You will learn more about fencing in the next section. Pasture gates need to be wide enough for a tractor or other farm equipment to get through. Fences and gates can be made of metal or wood. A horse shouldn't be able to put her leg between the rails of the fence.

Health

If left in pastures continuously, older horses, ponies, and certain breeds may develop a condition called metabolic syndrome. This health issue could lead to laminitis, a painful condition. You will learn more on these and other disorders in chapter 8. Talk to your horse's previous owner and your vet before pasturing your horse or pony.

Barbed wire, rusty metal gates, and rails can severely injure your horse. Have someone help you inspect any turnout area where you plan to keep your horse.

Pen Me In

If you don't have a pasture or your horse cannot be on grass full-time, you can keep her at home in a smaller pen or paddock with a shelter. The pen may or may not have grass, and it should be large enough to walk, trot, and canter in. It can be rectangular, oval, or round and made from a variety of materials. In this section, you'll learn some advantages and disadvantages to keeping your horse in this type of space.

All the advantages of keeping your horse at home on a pasture also apply to a home paddock. An additional advantage is that your property can be smaller. Paddocks are less expensive than pastures to keep up because they need less maintenance if they are set up and managed properly. Some boarding facilities also offer paddock and shelter options as an alternative to having your horse stabled in a barn.

There are many options for safe horse enclosures. The most effective—but also the most expensive— option is wooden posts and rails. Electric wire or tape attached inside the fence rails discourages horses from chewing on the wood, sticking their heads through the rails, and fighting with horses in nearby areas. The electric wire delivers a shock and should be checked regularly and carefully by a knowledgeable person. This shock discourages horses from undesirable behavior, but it doesn't hurt them. Paddock gates should be wide enough for a horse, wheelbarrow, or other manure-collecting containers to pass through.

Mud management is a disadvantage of paddock care if you live in a rainy area. Excessive mud can quickly become a health hazard for your horse. He can slip and fall or develop sores on his legs from standing in mud too long. Gravel for drainage and large, heavy rubber mats can be placed inside the shelter and through the gate entrance. These areas, where horses frequently stand or pace during feeding, tend to form hollows where water can collect and make mud puddles. If you plan on boarding your horse at a facility in a paddock, visit different places to see how muddy the paddocks are before moving your horse in.

Other disadvantages to keeping your horse at home in a paddock are manure, fly, and odor management. The smaller the space, the more often you'll need to remove the manure and soiled hay. Keep your manure pile far away from any houses to avoid odor, flies, and unhappy neighbors. Check with the local conservation district for guidance on mud and manure management.

If you keep more than one horse at home, use extreme caution when placing them in any space together, especially during feeding time. Unless the horses are longtime buddies, they'll need room to sort out their herd positions. One horse may corner, kick, or injure another. Have a horse expert help you before putting any horse at risk.

 "Corral" is a Western-style term for a pen or enclosure where cowboys place one or more horses that get along with each other.

You're Stalling

What's the difference between a barn and a stable? The terms are often used interchangeably to describe a farm or ranch building that houses livestock and/or farm equipment and tools. In this section, we'll use the word "stable" to refer to the structure and the word "stall" to refer to the space where a horse lives. You'll learn the advantages and disadvantages of stalling your horse at home or at another location and how to keep your horse safe in this type of space.

Stalls are usually square or rectangular. The size of your horse will determine the size of the stall he needs. Your horse needs to have enough room to lie down, roll, and turn. Smaller horses and ponies need smaller stalls, while draft horses and pregnant mares need larger ones.

Stalls are usually made of metal or wood, and they must be sturdy. Walls, bars, latches, and doors must be inspected regularly for sharp edges, protruding objects, or loose hinges. Large buckets with handles can be attached to strong wall hooks as long as the hooks don't pose a risk to the horse's eyes or face when she lowers her head in to eat or drink. Mangers or hay nets keep hay off the ground where the horse may soil it with manure or urine.

If your horse lives in a stall, you'll need to provide bedding. There are many types of bedding. Some examples are small wood chips or shavings, straw, and compact pellets. The most important considerations when choosing bedding are absorption, dust control, and warmth for when it is chilly.

The stall floor can be dirt or concrete. It should be level with good drainage, so urine can drain away from where the horse lies down. Large rubber mats are placed tightly together to allow for drainage and prevent slipping.

Stalling your horse at home has advantages. It is less expensive than paying others for the daily cleaning a stall requires to keep your horse healthy. Another plus is having a space for your horse that protects her in severe weather events like snow and rainstorms. Your horse can stay in a stall for days at a time, but she may become quite excitable when she finally gets to go outside. Ask for help when handling an energetic horse.

One disadvantage to stalling your horse is that it doesn't allow him to move and roam around. Horses need exercise every day, either by **lunging**, riding, or daily turnout in a paddock or pasture. Lunging is when a horse circles around an experienced person holding a long rope or line. Horses can walk, trot, and canter on a long enough line.

If your horse lives at home, you can spend more time with her and put her in a paddock or pasture every day to exercise. If she is boarded, you'll have to travel every day to turn her out if you are caring for her, or you'll need to pay someone to turn her out.

 A 1,000-pound horse eliminates an average of 60 to 70 pounds of stall waste every day. That adds up to a lot of mucking!

Stable Living

You've learned about different horse homes and the benefits of each. Now, we'll talk about the advantages and disadvantages of boarding your horse in a stable, where other people take care of your horse and there are a number of services you can use to have fun with your **equine** partner.

First, do your homework and visit many stables in your area. Looking at the different stables will help you determine what the most important elements are in choosing your horse's home. Find the closest stable you can afford so that you can visit often.

The cost of boarding stables varies greatly and depends on many factors, such as the size of the facility, location, conveniences, and the services they offer. Large facilities may offer conveniences such as indoor and outdoor riding and training year-round in small and large spaces called arenas. Arenas may sound like an advantage, but they're expensive to maintain. It requires lighting and routine care to keep the arenas safe and useable.

Location may affect the cost, depending on where the facility is located. The more expensive the neighborhood, the more expensive it is to board. Facilities tend to be less expensive in rural areas.

If the stable is a performance facility, it may offer services such as riding lessons in a specific activity, like jumping. Some facilities require that you take lessons or have your horse in training. Other expenses to consider are transportation and horse-show fees.

If you are boarding at a non-competitive riding stable, riding lessons and horse training may be optional rather than required. Remember, your horse's care is your responsibility even when he is kept away from home.

Sweet Dreams

Horses can sleep standing up so they can run from danger at a moment's notice. Horses have a special ability to lock their legs so they can relax their muscles and doze off without falling over. But that doesn't mean horses always sleep standing up—they need to lie down for deep sleep at least some of the time.

CHAPTER

7

Grooming Guide

Whether your horse is at home or boarded, grooming is an important part of her daily care. It may even prevent visits from the vet. In this chapter, you'll learn the benefits of grooming and the tools and techniques you'll use for shows and **competitions**.

Monitoring and preventing health problems is important for your horse's overall well-being. Grooming your horse increases blood flow to the skin's surface, massages large muscle groups, and keeps her feet free of harmful debris. It's also great exercise for you.

While grooming your horse, you may notice new bumps, scrapes, scratches, or sensitive areas before they become serious problems. If your horse's body language indicates he's not happy during grooming, ask for help so you can discover the problem and work on fixing it.

Horses become comfortable around humans who perform tasks that feel good. Grooming time is an opportunity for you and your horse to bond. And grooming is just plain fun!

The first part of grooming is learning the names of the tools and how to use them. We'll cover additional tools in later sections. Let's start grooming!

Tool Time

Here is a list of common tools used to keep your equine friend clean, happy, and healthy.

Plastic/Rubber Curry Comb

This tool is used first to remove shedding hair, dried sweat, and mud. Use brisk circular motions to loosen the debris and follow up with the dandy brush.

Rubber Grooming Mitt

Like the curry comb, this tool is used for removing debris, but it is most useful on the legs and head. Use gentle strokes over these bony parts of the horse.

Dandy Brush

This stiff brush has long bristles and is used for removing body stains and dirt brought up from the curry comb. Use quick flicks across the body.

Body Brush

This brush has soft bristles. Using long strokes, polish the coat and use cautiously on ticklish areas near the horse's flanks and belly. Then follow with the stable cloth for extra shine.

Stable Cloth or Rubber

This tool can be made from an old clean rag, towel, or washcloth. Dampen the cloth, then use it to clean around the eyes, ears, and nose.

Currying your horse every day brings the oils in the skin to the surface. Remember to curry and brush in the same direction the hair grows in.

Face Brush

This small brush has soft bristles for the sensitive areas of the head, such as the forehead, ears, jaw, chin, and throatlatch areas. Use this tool after the body grooming.

Mane Comb

Use your fingers and a mane detangler before using the wide-tooth mane comb. Use this tool with care so the mane hair does not break or pull.

Hoof Pick

This tool is used to gently pick out debris from the horse's hooves. This task is usually last and is an important step in health care.

Shedding Blade

This tool has sharp teeth. Be very careful while using it on your horse's coat. The shedding blade helps remove shedding hair more quickly.

Sponge

Sponges come in different sizes for a variety of uses. Large sponges are good for bathing larger areas, while smaller ones work well for washing faces.

Sweat Scraper

This tool can be plastic, metal, or rubber. It scrapes off excess water after bathing or sweat after a workout.

 If it's too cold to bathe your horse, use a sponge and warm water to wipe off her face, neck, saddle, and girth area.

Water Brush

This wooden-backed tool is softer than the dandy and is used to wet down the mane and tail. It may come with an attached sponge.

Metal Curry Comb

This tool has largely been replaced by the softer rubber curry combs. It is a great tool for removing the hair from your dandy brush.

Tail or Mane Brush

To prevent hair breakage, this tool should be made of a non-metal material. You can use a human hairbrush or buy one specifically for horses.

The Mane Thing

Caring for your horse's mane and tail is an important task for her overall health. Some equine sporting events or shows require a certain look for the mane and tail, and your horse is judged based on how she looks.

Before getting started, practice safety by asking for help. Introduce your horse to the space, ties, and stepping stool you may need to climb on to reach her mane. Check with your riding instructor about the mane and tail requirements for your chosen activity. Then learn how to do the following tasks yourself.

Braided

Braided manes were originally a status symbol, but they also prevented reins from tangling while riding. Modern riders in horse shows and competitions use a variety of braid styles, from simple to decorative. Braiding is fun and shows off your skills while making your horse look extra special and loved. Remember to start with a groomed mane.

Braids can be simple, like the common three-strand, or fancy, like the diamond-braided long mane. Start by practicing the three-strand braid. This braid can be done on short and long manes. Remember to keep this grooming activity fun and safe.

Banded

Banded manes are typically done for Western shows. A banded mane is a nice finishing touch that makes the neck look slimmer. Showmanship, halter, trail, and horsemanship are some of the classes where you will see this style of mane.

Using a mane comb, start with a damp, clean, shortened, even mane. Evenly divide the mane into small sections. Use clips to hold each section and wind a rubber band tightly around the lock of hair near the crest of the neck.

Pulled

Pulled manes have been shortened to a desired length by pulling the hair out by the roots. These manes are easier to manage, decorative for shows, and functional during equine sporting events. Some breeds have neck shapes that look better when the mane is shortened. In English events, the mane is pulled so it can be braided in the appropriate style for competing safely or stylishly.

Some horse owners use special tools such as thinning shears, combs, or clippers instead of pulling the mane from the roots. Ask for help in selecting the right tool so your horse continues to trust you.

Roached

Roached or hogged manes have been completely removed. Roaching is done using clippers or shears. There are sporting events, breed-show requirements, and health reasons for roaching the mane. In South America, the manes are roached so that ticks can be seen easily and removed quickly.

Before roaching your horse's mane, remember you are removing her natural fly control. Roaching the mane is not painful, but, like pulling a mane, it must be done every four to six weeks to keep the desired length.

Thinned

Some horses and ponies have extremely thick manes and tails that are difficult and time-consuming to pull and tangle easily. Simple braiding is one option for these manes. This solution requires frequent re-braiding so the braided hair does not shear off during turnout. Other horses may see these braids as tasty morsels and chew on them.

Another option is to thin the mane. Thinning is different from shortening. When thinning a mane, you divide the mane into a top and underneath part. Then, using thinning shears or clippers, you cut the underneath part close to the crest. To maintain this look, you must trim the mane every four to six weeks.

The Best Braids

Evenly divide a small section of mane into three equal parts. Hold the inside and outside pieces, leaving the middle section hanging down.

Using your thumb and forefinger to grab the middle section, cross each of the other sections, alternating until you reach the end.

Bind each braid with a rubber band and repeat.

Pony Tails

In this section, you'll learn about tail care. Ask for help to position yourself safely while working around the back end of your horse.

Braided

The three-strand braid is the most common braid for managing or growing long tails. There are many styles and reasons for braiding the tail. When tails drag on the ground, horses can step on them, drag them through mud, or catch them on objects. Some classes of Western-style and gaited horses have long tails and need to be carefully groomed. Braiding, and often bandaging, protects long tails from damage.

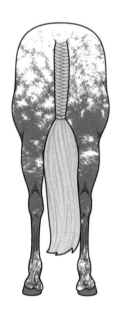

   Decorative braids such as the French, Dutch, and hunter braids are seen in English shows. Braiding is fun, and with practice, you could have the best-looking horse in the stable.

Banged

The banged tail is a technique of cutting the end of the tail in such a way that the ends are neatly shortened. Do not cut it straight across or it will appear uneven. English- and Western-style riders have certain preferences for the length of the tail. Always check with other riders or your riding instructor before shortening the tail.

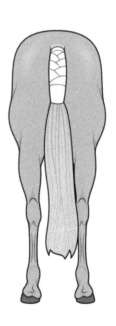

Ask for experienced help before trying to shorten a horse's tail for the first time. Your horse may be ticklish or nervous at first. You may need to go slowly so your horse is relaxed.

Bandaged

Herringbone tail bandages are often used to prevent a horse from rubbing its tail hairs off on walls, fences, or other objects. These bandages keep the horse's tail clean in muddy conditions and protect braided tails during transportation and overnight for horse shows. Veterinarians may use bandaging during exams and procedures when the tail is in the way.

Bandages must be applied correctly to be safe and effective. The herringbone pattern prevents excess pressure on the blood vessels in the dock of the tail. If the bandage is applied too tightly, it can severely injure the tail. Ask for professional help when bandaging the tail.

 Violin bows have more than 150 hairs from the tail of a horse. Members of the violin family with wider ribbons use even more hairs.

Clippety-Clip

Clipping may be necessary if you exercise your horse regularly or compete during colder months of the year. Horses grow thicker coats for the winter, so it may be harder to cool and dry them after a strenuous workout or competition. Having your horse wear blankets as the weather becomes cooler can prevent heavy hair growth, but some horses and ponies grow thicker coats year-round.

You can use electric clippers to remove excess hair over some areas or over the whole body. The type of clipping pattern you choose may depend on the time of year and the type of work or competition you do. Have an expert help you decide if your horse will benefit from clipping. Ask for help before trying to use noisy, vibrating clippers on your horse. Some clippers are quieter, cordless, and rechargeable. The rechargeable ones are handy when a power source isn't available. The most common clipping patterns are full clip, trace clip, and blanket clip.

Clipping takes patience, practice, and expert help until you and your horse are confident. Before clipping, make sure your clippers are clean, oiled, and fitted with a sharp blade. Choose a safe space and arrange your tools. If your clippers have a cord, ask an expert to show you how to move around your horse safely.

Remember, be patient while working with your horse. You are both learning, and your job is to maintain the hard-earned trust he has in you.

Bath Time

Horses have natural skin oils that provide a barrier against the environment, regulate body temperature, and promote healthy bacteria. Frequent shampooing can disturb this balance and cause health problems. Most experts say two to three baths a year is enough. You can rinse more often for removing sweat. Ask an experienced horse person to help the first time.

Wet the Entire Horse

Use a gentle stream of water and slowly start from the hooves up to get your horse used to the water and temperature.

Shampoo and Scrub

Using a large sponge, shampoo and scrub one section at a time. Use small wet sponges without shampoo when bathing the face and other delicate areas.

Rinse Thoroughly

Rinse each area thoroughly before moving on. Start rinsing at the top of a section, like the horse's shoulder, and work your way down.

Condition and Detangle

Use a conditioner or detangler on the mane and tail to make combing easier. Rinse thoroughly until the suds are gone.

Scrape and Dry

Dry your horse starting with the sweat scraper to remove as much water as possible. Then use towels to absorb any remaining dampness.

Brush the Mane and Tail

Finish the bath by drying the mane and tail. Use your fingers to separate the hairs before gently running the mane comb or brush through.

Trimming a Bridle Path

The bridle path is located behind the ears. Horses and ponies with thicker manes need a bridle path to keep the mane from tangling in the halter or bridle. With help, use shears or clippers to keep this area clipped regularly to maintain a nice look.

Blanket Basics

In the wild, horses don't need blankets. They seek shelter from weather, huddle together for warmth, or use their tails to swat flies off each other. Horses have adapted to the areas they live in over a long period by growing heavy or thin coats.

Although many horses do fine without blankets, domestic horses wear blankets for many reasons. When we bathe, clip, and keep horses indoors, their bodies need protection from the environmental elements. Before buying a blanket, ask an expert to help you decide whether your horse needs one and, if so, what type and size. In this section, you'll learn about the different types of blankets and what they're used for.

Cooler

The material used for this blanket wicks or absorbs moisture. Coolers can be used for warming up before a workout or cooling down after one.

Sheet

Stable sheets are lightweight and breathable, and keep the horse clean. They provide a light layer of warmth while indoors and outdoors.

Fly Sheet

These lightweight fly protection blankets are made from woven material that is breathable and resists tearing. They can partially or fully cover the horse.

Winter Blanket

These are thicker blankets designed to keep your horse warm. They can be waterproof for wearing outside or intended for inside use only.

Turnout Blanket

These are tough, waterproof blankets that resist rubs and tears when worn outside. They come with or without lining for warmth and comfort.

Learn proper care for the blanket you choose. Waterproof blankets need to be checked regularly and re-waterproofed. Otherwise your horse may become chilled and ill.

Don't Forget

Know Your Ticklish Areas

Be careful when grooming ticklish areas, such as your horse's flank or belly. Place your empty hand firmly on her side or hindquarters to reassure her.

Bony Areas Are Sensitive

For your horse's comfort and grooming pleasure, use softer tools over bony horse parts and stiffer brushes and tools over well-muscled areas. Your horse will appreciate it!

Bend at the Knees

While grooming your horse's legs, bend at the knees rather than kneeling or sitting. If your horse moves suddenly, you can get out of the way more easily.

Prepare Before You Bathe

Before bathing your horse, groom and remove dirt and excess hair. Gather your tools in a bucket and place the bucket away from his legs.

Ask for Help

Ask for help from an experienced horse person when introducing your horse to new activities such as clipping, bathing, or mane and tail care.

CHAPTER

8

Healthy and Happy

Do you want your horse to live a long, healthy, happy life? Of course, you do! That's why preventive care is so important. Preventive care is when you practice routine activities to prevent your horse from becoming sick.

Preventive care includes vaccinations, deworming, hoof care, dental care, and daily care. Your vet can help you schedule a deworming, vaccination, and dental plan. Your farrier can help you schedule hoof care. Daily care is what you do for your horse. When you check your horse every day, you can detect early signs of illness or injury and notify the appropriate professional.

Veterinarians and farriers are your professional partners in helping you develop and maintain a preventive health-care plan for your horse. They will also be the ones you call when something changes.

To find a vet and farrier, start by asking horse people you know or people at your boarding facility. If you keep your horse at home, find nearby professionals who can come quickly in an emergency. Post their phone numbers on your horse's stall or where they can easily be seen.

In this chapter, you'll learn about your horse's health needs and how to keep him at his best.

Daily Dose

Checking your horse every day will help you notice any new issues or problems early. In this section, you'll learn a few important daily tasks that will help you watch for changes and know what to do if you notice them. Anytime you are in doubt or do not have a horse expert to ask, call your vet.

These are the things you should check every day:

Water

Wash and refill your horse's water, noting any changes in the amount she usually drinks. If she stops drinking for more than a day, call your vet.

Manure

Your horse's manure should be formed into moist balls. If the manure is too dry or too wet, your horse may have a digestive problem. Ask an expert to help you decide if you need to call the vet.

Appetite

Appetite change could be an early sign of illness. Monitor how much your horse is eating or what he is not eating and report these changes to the vet.

Energy Level

Pay attention to how high or low your horse's energy level is normally. A change in your horse's energy level may be a sign of early illness. Call your vet and report the changes.

Injuries

Look for new scrapes, cuts, or puncture wounds on your horse's legs, head, and body. Treat any injuries promptly and be sure to ask for help with treatment.

Lameness

While exercising your horse or while riding, notice any changes in her gaits. If you feel like she is walking irregularly or limping, have your vet evaluate her.

Illness

A runny nose, coughing, or wheezing should be reported to the boarding facility and vet immediately. Your horse should be separated from other horses until the vet examines him.

 Any changes in behavior could mean there's a problem. Write down and report to the vet what you see, hear, smell, or feel and what has changed.

Hoof Care

Place hoof care near the top of your daily horse care list. Most hoof problems can be prevented with routine care. In this section, you'll learn four ways to care for your horse's hooves and when to report changes to your farrier.

Cleaning

Regular hoof cleaning is an important part of keeping your horse healthy and happy. Using the hoof pick, lift the foot and pick gently around the frog and on the sole. Loosen and remove any rocks, sticks, manure, or debris. Hoof cleaning should be done whether you ride or not.

Trimming

Horses need to be trimmed every four to seven weeks to maintain a healthy hoof and foot that is free from chipping, cracking, and soreness. Many horses have strong hooves and can be ridden without shoes. Have a skilled professional trim your horse's feet rather than doing it yourself.

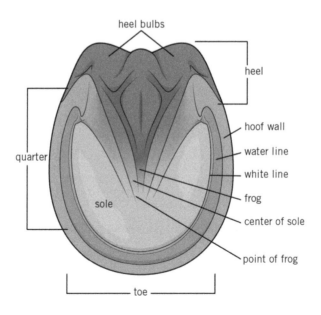

heel bulbs

heel

hoof wall

water line

white line

frog

center of sole

point of frog

quarter

sole

toe

Shoeing

Horseshoes protect the bottom of the horse's feet from chipping and becoming sore. Shoeing is a job for the farrier. He or she will shape and apply the shoes after trimming the hooves properly. The farrier uses steel nails to attach the shoe to the hoof and keep it in place. Shoeing does not hurt the horse.

Boots

Horse boots are another option for hoof care. They're like the shoes you wear. Horse boots come in a variety of shapes and sizes and are fitted to your horse after he's been trimmed. Boots are used for horses that do well barefoot but need extra protection on trails with sharp rocks.

Dental Care

Routine dental care by a qualified vet is an important part of keeping your horse healthy. Unlike your teeth, your horse's teeth keep growing throughout most of her life, especially in the early years. Front teeth are called **incisors** and cut grass. Back teeth, called **molars**, grind the forage and grains. The average horse needs her teeth checked every year. The vet will also float your horse's teeth when needed. **Floating** means filing or rasping the teeth to keep the molar chewing surfaces level, as well as rounding off sharp edges and possibly removing troublesome **wolf teeth**. Some horses may need more dental attention than others and require more frequent visits.

Wolf teeth are small, shallow-rooted teeth that grow in front of the permanent molars in young horses. Removing these teeth decreases pain and pressure from the bit.

Begin dental care when your horse is young to identify and correct potential problems. Watch for signs that she may need her teeth examined. She may stop eating or drop wads of grass or hay while she is eating. She may toss her head when a bit is placed in her mouth or rub her mouth on her leg or fences. These could be signs of discomfort.

If your horse is older, she may need extra dental care. At this stage of the life cycle, the teeth stop growing and eventually wear down to the gums. Teeth can also change height and angle as they move outward. This change can lead to uneven wear that makes it difficult for your horse to fully grind her food, which affects her digestion. Notify your regular vet or a dental specialist as soon as possible if you suspect pain or if you need your horse examined.

Emergency Kit

Always keep first-aid supplies marked and in an easy-to-find location when you are away. Buy a basic kit with supplies for minor injuries or illnesses from an equine-supply company. Ask an experienced horse person or vet to help you use the supplies.

Pest Control

Pests and parasites are insects, worms, bacteria, and fungi that can live inside or on your horse's body. Some pests and parasites can cause serious illness.

Some insects crawl on the skin or fly and land on your horse, biting, sucking blood, or laying eggs on the horse's hair. These eggs hatch and create more parasites and pests. Biting insects can carry diseases that could make your horse ill and cause permanent damage. Mosquitoes and some horseflies may be seen in swarms around your horse. Some parasites are so small you cannot see them at all. In this section, you will learn about different pests and parasites, what signs to look for, and how to treat your horse.

Worms

Worms are parasites living inside your horse. They can cause serious health problems if not managed properly. Prevention of worm infestation is the best practice. Infestation means that a large number of worms are present and must be treated immediately. Weight loss, poor appetite, liquid manure, and low energy could be signs of worm infestation. Ask your vet to set up the best worm-prevention plan and teach you how to administer the medicine. Medicine is often given by mouth as a paste or gel. Ask for expert help when giving any medicine to your horse.

Bot Flies

Bot flies lay small yellow-orange eggs on horses' legs in warmer months. Ask for expert help when removing the eggs and administering the treatment. Ask your vet which medicine is best and when to give it to prevent this parasite from making your horse ill.

Horseflies

These large biting insects attach painfully on your horse's skin and feast on her blood. Applying fly spray in the summer is often an effective prevention.

Stable Flies

These swarming flies hang around your horse's eyes, nose, and mouth. They are found in and near manure, where they are busy laying eggs. Buy a fly mask and ask for help to place it on your horse's head. This mask keeps the pests away from your horse's eyes.

Ticks

These small blood-sucking insects cause a variety of diseases and are more common in some places. Ticks are difficult to see on darker horses and require an expert to remove. Some fly sprays have an added ingredient that keeps these pests from bothering your horse.

Fungus

Like bacteria, fungus can infect your horse's skin and cause it to become itchy and irritated. A vet can test for fungus and treat it with specific medicated solutions that you can spray on your horse or bathe him with.

Mites

These insects live on the skin and cause an itchy, crusty skin condition called mange. The vet will test for mites and provide the treatment.

Lice

These tiny parasitic insects live in the horse's coat and cause itchy, irritated skin. As with mites, the vet will need to test for these parasites and provide the treatment.

Mosquitoes

Mosquitoes like to bite your horse as much as they like to bite you. Ask your vet if your horse needs specific vaccinations to protect him from mosquito diseases in your area. Choose a fly spray that prevents mosquitoes as well as flies.

 Routinely removing manure from areas where horses eat or graze decreases the presence of pests and parasites. Have your vet check a manure sample for worms every year.

Vaccines

Good preventive care includes a vaccination plan. Vaccinations protect your horse from developing or catching common horse illnesses. Some common vaccines given to horses are **influenza (flu)**, **rhino**, and **tetanus** vaccines. The rhino vaccine prevents the virus that causes colds. Both flu and rhino are contagious. Tetanus is a serious illness for humans and horses caused by bacteria. Tetanus is not contagious, and the vaccine needs to be given more often for horses than humans.

Ask your vet which vaccinations are recommended in your area and how often they should be given. If you plan on taking your horse to other locations for horse shows or competitions, find out which vaccinations are required before you go. Check with your vet if you are planning to cross state lines. Other states may require specific vaccinations, blood tests, and health certificates.

Different regions have higher risks for certain infections. Your vet is the best resource and will give the shots your horse needs. Keep an accurate record of all your horse's health care, including the dates and types of vaccines. This record is a great way to track and monitor your horse's health care.

Common Problems

In this section, you'll learn about common problems you may see in horses. Knowing what to look for in advance can help you recognize and treat the conditions.

Rain Scald

This contagious bacterial infection affects the skin on the upper areas of the horse's back, head, and shoulders, causing scabby, crusty bumps. The hair falls out in patches, leaving bald spots. Treat the affected areas with antibacterial shampoos and rinses made for horses. Treat daily until the skin is healed.

Ringworm

Ringworm is not a worm but a contagious fungal infection that lives on the skin. It causes loss of hair in round patches. Unlike other horse infections, ringworm is contagious to other animals and humans. Isolate your horse and call your vet. The vet will test for ringworm, confirm the infection, and provide the proper treatment.

Mud Fever

Also known as scratches, this infection can be caused by bacteria, fungi, or both. Mud fever will spread if not treated. It affects the legs or lower part of the body, causing raw, oozing sores. Mud fever also causes hair to fall off in patches. This infection needs to be treated with antibacterial shampoo and rinses until it is gone.

Strangles

This highly contagious bacterial infection is like human mumps. Strangles affects the lymph nodes under the horse's jaw. A horse with strangles can quickly infect an entire stable of horses. Isolate your horse as soon as possible to stop the infection from spreading. Call the vet immediately.

Thrush

This hoof infection is caused by fungus or bacteria and can become a chronic condition if left untreated. The organisms eat away at the frog and cause a rotten, sour smell that you'll notice when picking the hoof. Treatment with antifungal ointments and keeping your horse in a clean, dry environment can help stop the infection.

Sweet Itch

This irritating skin condition is caused by an allergy to midges during the spring and fall. Midges are small biting flies that can cause an allergic reaction. Horses can become so itchy that they can rub their mane and tail hair off and rub their bellies raw. Call the vet for treatment.

Colic

If your horse is repeatedly getting up and down to roll, sweating, and biting at his sides, this could be a life-and-death condition called colic. Colic is a problem in the digestive tract that can have a number of causes. Remain calm and call the vet immediately.

Laminitis

Finding the cause of this painful hoof condition is important for providing the right treatment. A common cause is too much green pasture grass. Front leg limping is a common sign. Remove the horse from the pasture and call the vet.

Lameness

Lameness is common and refers to a horse limping due to discomfort or pain in one or more legs. Lameness can be caused by many conditions, so have a vet check the sore leg or hoof to discover the location and provide the right treatment.

Horses roll for pleasure and fun, especially after a bath. They like dry sand best so they can scratch their backs and sides.

CHAPTER

9

Sports, Shows, and FUN!

When your horse is happy and healthy, there are many activities the two of you can do together. There are competitive and non-competitive equestrian activities to learn about before you decide what fits you and your horse best.

Competitive equestrian sports are activities you do while riding your horse or being pulled by your horse in a carriage or cart. You and your horse compete with other equestrians in events, games, or shows. These can be team sports or individual riding sports. Equestrian sports hold competitions, events, or horse shows and have rules that you must follow to enter and win a competition.

In this chapter, we'll explore different equestrian sports. Make sure you have a veterinarian, horse trainer, and/or riding instructor help you choose the right sport that keeps you and your horse safe, healthy, and happy.

What Sport?

How do you know what kind of activity is right for you? First, let's start with choosing a style.

If you choose Western style and prefer slower competitions, you might choose showmanship, horsemanship, or trail classes. If you prefer a faster speed, you might choose rodeo activities like barrel racing, roping, reining, or mounted games.

If you choose English style and prefer slower competitions, you might choose dressage, vaulting, hunter-jumper, or equitation. If you prefer a faster speed, you might choose polo, cross-country, endurance riding, show jumping, harness, or flat racing.

In non-competitive equestrian activities, you can choose either style of gear and ride on trails with family and friends or take riding lessons. You can join a local 4-H or Pony Club in your area to learn horse care, horsemanship, and preparations for competitions or shows.

Here's more about the fun activities you can do with your horse.

Hacking

English-style riders use this term to describe riding a horse on trails or roads at average speeds. The purpose of hacking is light exercise and pleasure for both horse and rider. Hacking is typically at a walk, trot, or canter.

Showing

Showing is a term used by both Western- and English-style competitors. It is a judged competition with a series of performances called classes. Classes have groups of horses that are similar in breed or training style. Hunter-jumper or jumping are some examples of classes. In some classes, the horses are judged on conformation—how well their physical features match the ideals of their breed—and obedience. In other classes, riders are judged on how well they ride. Prizes can be ribbons, money, trophies, or a combination of these.

In 2016, California Chrome became the highest-earning Thoroughbred with a total of $12 million in earnings at one horse race. That'll buy a lot of carrots!

Dressage

Dressage is an English-style riding activity. It is considered a sport, a competition, and an art. The term is used to describe a highly trained, relaxed horse and rider. The rider memorizes and completes predetermined movements, such as the working trot or the extended trot. The rider and horse advance through levels of training that become increasingly difficult.

Show Jumping

Show jumping is a fast, English-style competition. The fastest horse-and-rider team that stays on a memorized course with the fewest faults wins. Faults are penalty points that are given when a horse knocks down a rail while jumping. There are also time faults, which are given when a team doesn't complete the course in the time set by its designer.

Jousting

Jousting was an ancient tournament that involved two armored riders galloping toward each other on either side of a barrier. Each rider was armed with a long spear called a lance. The first knight to touch the other was awarded points. Jousting is now done for entertainment only.

Hunter–Jumping

This English-style competition judges the horse's style and ability as a hunting horse. In the past, foxes were hunted by riders on horseback who brought hunting dogs to find the fox. A horse competing in hunter-jumping must have smooth and consistent gaits while completing a course with jumps. Jumping is judged on accuracy, grace, and form. This sport is more stylized, with special grooming, tack, and equipment for both horse and rider.

Equitation classes judge the equestrian's riding skills in the hunting seat and jumping seat. These classes were designed to prepare a rider for hunter-jumping competitions.

Mounted Games

This fast, English-style mounted sport has competitions for people of all ages on horses up to 15 hands tall. This sport is divided into games for teams, pairs, and individuals. The games feature tasks such as carton races and flag fliers, and they require a high level of riding skill and partnership with your horse.

Cross-Country Event

This fast, English-style jumping sport is part of a three-day event. On the jumping day, the horse and rider compete on an uneven field course alone and jump over a set number of obstacles within a fixed time. They get point penalties for going over time or if a horse refuses to jump an obstacle.

Endurance Riding

This equestrian sport is for riders who love speed and well-marked trails. Races can be 25 to 100 miles long and may require camping overnight. Some riders do this sport as a personal challenge. Pairs ride solo and are judged on time and the horse's condition along the way.

The three-day event is an equestrian contest that has trials in dressage, cross-country, and stadium jumping. The same horse and rider complete all three trials.

Competitive Trail Riding

This sport is like endurance riding but not quite as fast. Riders follow a marked trail for a predetermined distance. As with endurance riding, the goal is to demonstrate close partnership between the horse and rider. Some riders start with this sport and later move into endurance riding.

Rodeo

A rodeo is a collection of unmounted and mounted Western-style contests. Cattle are used in roping, sorting, wrestling, and cutting contests. Other contests include barrel racing, tie-down, and team roping. Most of these contests are judged on speed and require a high level of fitness and practice on and off the horse.

Polo

This mounted English-style sport is played by teams at high speed. The object of the game is to hit a ball through goal posts with a mallet. Think of polo as hockey on horseback. Riders and horses must be athletic and work as a team. Riders must be able to swing a mallet quickly with both hands.

Mounted Archery

This ancient sport involves using bows and arrows to shoot at targets while riding a horse. Mounted archery requires a great deal of knowledge and practice. The rider must be skilled at archery before trying to shoot while mounted. Archers must also be able to ride their horses at all four gaits without using their hands.

Horseball

This English-style team sport is like polo, football, and basketball all in one. It is a fast, mounted competition where a ball is carried by hand and shot through a high net to score points. During the competition, riders use the weight of their horses to shove their opponents out of the playing area without unseating themselves.

 To escape danger, the average horse gallops 25 to 30 miles per hour. The world record was 55 miles per hour at a short distance.

Flat Racing

This ancient, fast sport involves riders called jockeys. A jockey is a rider who is lightweight, which allows the horse to go faster. Special saddles are needed so that the jockeys can ride as low as possible. In the United States, Thoroughbreds, American Quarter Horses, and Arabians are raced and can earn their owners money.

Working Cow Horse

This Western-style competition tests the rider and horse on their ability to maneuver and control one cow. During cow work, the horse is judged by cow sense, smoothness, manners, and ease of reining—how easy it is for the rider to maneuver the horse.

Vaulting

Vaulting combines gymnastics with dance on the back of a horse. Riders are called vaulters and compete as a team in gymnastic-style clothes. Horses are placed on a long rope and circle a trainer in the middle as vaulters pace alongside the horse and mount while the horse is in motion.

Best Friends for Life

Now that you have learned about choosing and caring for the perfect horse and you've picked the activity you would like to do with your new partner, you can dream of one day owning that horse. With careful planning, a lot of knowledge, and experts to guide you, you'll find the perfect horse that is out there waiting for you.

If you already own a horse, I hope this guide helped you learn more about caring for your equine friend. Meanwhile, take riding lessons, help at a stable, lease a horse, and learn as much as you can from all the horses you meet along the way. Have a great horse life!

Routines to Follow

Daily

Use this handy list to remember the basic tasks your horse needs every day:

- Provide fresh water and quality forage.
- Check the hay for mold and debris as you feed.
- Feed grains, vitamins, and minerals if required.
- Check the salt block.
- Provide a safe stall or shelter.
- Clean the stall or shelter by removing manure and urine.
- Remove manure from small paddocks.
- Wipe out the grain bucket to keep rats and flies away.
- Add more bedding as needed.
- Check the stall or shelter for sharp objects.
- Check the pasture and paddock for unsafe debris and fallen trees.
- Put all tools in a safe area away from your horse.
- Check and replace damaged stable tools.
- Check your horse for new scrapes or injuries.
- Clean your horse's hooves.

- Notice signs of illness, like a runny nose or coughing.
- When using a blanket, check for tangled or loose straps.
- Check the fences and gates for damage to wood or wire.
- Remove large rocks from the paddock.
- Turn your horse out.
- Check any rubber mats for overlapping.
- Provide an area for your horse to avoid standing in mud.
- Spend fun time with your horse.
- Clean or wipe down your tack and grooming tools after each use.
- Check tack and gear for damage and replace if needed.

Weekly

The following chores need to be done every week:

- Hand graze if there is no access to pasture.
- Exercise your horse during groundwork or riding.
- Empty, scrub, and refill water containers in paddocks and pastures.
- Remove manure from pastures or smaller fields.
- Thoroughly groom your horse, including its mane and tail.

Occasionally

Check with your vet, farrier, and riding instructor to decide how often to do these items:

- Check and replace any missing items in the first-aid kit.
- Strip the stall or shelter area and use a hose to clean the mats.
- Apply fly repellent as recommended on the label.
- Deworm your horse on a schedule set up by your vet.
- Set up routine hoof care with your farrier.
- Bathe your horse as recommended by your riding instructor.
- Clip your horse for shows as recommended.
- Clean your blankets and saddle pads.
- Check waterproof blankets by feeling your horse's skin for moisture.
- Clean or replace grooming tools when damaged.
- Clean or replace damaged tack and gear.
- Check your helmet to make sure it continues to fit as you grow.
- Check with your vet and vaccinate as needed when traveling.

Yearly

There are only a few things you need to do each year, but they are important:

- Schedule a yearly vet visit for a wellness check and vaccinations.
- Have the vet float your horse's teeth every six months or yearly, as needed.

Glossary

aid: The body language or tool a rider uses to signal to the horse to perform a task or movement

band: A group of horses in the wild that is led by a dominant mare

beat: One or more of a horse's feet hitting the ground within a gait

behavior: The desirable or undesirable actions or reactions of a horse

breed: A kind of horse that was developed for a certain purpose and has similar characteristics to others within the same group

broodmare: A female horse kept for having foals

cereal grain: The seeds that come from grasses, such as wheat, barley, oats, and corn, that are typically fed to horses and called grain

characteristics: Features or qualities shared by members of a group that uniquely identify them as belonging to that group

colt: A male horse under the age of three

competition: A horse event, show, or contest

crossbred: When horses of specific breeds are bred with each other to produce a mixed-breed foal

dam: A female parent of a foal

equestrian: Related to horseback-riding activities, or a name for someone who rides horses

equine: A horse or another member of the horse family

farrier: A horse expert who trims and shoes horses and often works with vets to treat hoof conditions

filly: A female horse under the age of three

floating: The dental procedure of filing or rasping the teeth to keep the molar chewing surfaces level and round off sharp edges

foal: A baby horse under the age of one

gait: The way a horse moves forward, including the four standard gaits—walk, trot, canter (or lope), and gallop

gelding: A castrated male horse

groundwork: Unmounted handling or training a horse for manners or in preparation to ride

herd: A group of horses sharing the same space

incisors: The front teeth used by horses for tearing grass

influenza (flu): An illness of the lungs caused by a virus

lead: In a canter, when the leg on the inside of a circle lands farther forward than the one on the outside of the circle

lunging: An exercise in which a horse, attached to a long rope or line, circles around a person

mare: A female horse over the age of three

molars: The back teeth that horses use to grind grain and forage

nutrient: A substance found in food that provides nourishment that's essential for growth and the maintenance of life

pony: A small type of horse

rhino: An illness of the lungs that is caused by a virus and is similar to the common cold

sire: A male parent of a foal

stallion: A male horse over the age of three

temperament: An animal's nature, especially as it affects behavior

tetanus: A bacterial infection in horses

type: A group of horses that share physical characteristics, temperament, and/or jobs

veterinarian (vet): The horse expert who helps with preventive health care and treats illnesses and conditions

weanling: A foal that has been separated from its mother and is no longer nursing

wolf teeth: The small, shallow-rooted teeth that erupt in front of the permanent molars in young horses

yearling: A horse that's between one and two years old

Resources

Websites

Allen Financial Insurance Group: Horse Safety Manual
www.eqgroup.com/library/horse_safety/

American Association of Equine Practitioners
www.aaep.org

American Horse Council
www.horsecouncil.org

EquiMed: Horse Health Matters
www.equimed.com

The Horse: Your Guide to Equine Healthcare
www.thehorse.com

Kentucky Equine Research
www.ker.com

National 4-H Council
www.4-h.org

The United States Pony Club
www.ponyclub.org

Books

Cherry Hill's Horse Care for Kids by Cherry Hill

Essential Horse Health: The Most Common Equine Health Problems Solved by Kieran O'Brien

Getting the Most from Riding Lessons by Mike Smith

Getting Your First Horse by Judith Dutson

Horse Crazy! 1,001 Fun Facts, Craft Projects, Games, Activities, and Know-How for Horse-Loving Kids by Jessie Haas

Horse Health Matters: The Horse Owner's Guide to Equine Healthcare by Mark Sellers and Flossie Sellers

Horse Sense: A Complete Guide to Horse Selection and Care by John J. Mettler Jr.

Natural Horse-Man-Ship: The Six Keys to a Natural Horse-Human Relationship by Pat Parelli

The New Book of Saddlery and Tack edited by Carolyn Henderson

References

Crisp, Marty. *Everything Horse: What Kids Really Want to Know about Horses.* Minnetonka, MN: Northword Press, 2005.

Draper, Judith, Debbie Sly, and Sarah Muir. *Complete Book of Horses and Riding.* New York: Anness Publishing, 2010.

Dutson, Judith. *Storey's Illustrated Guide to 96 Horse Breeds of North America.* North Adams, MA: Storey Publishing, 2005.

Edwards, Elwyn Hartley. *The New Encyclopedia of the Horse.* New York: Dorling Kindersley, 2001.

Getty, Juliet M. *Feed Your Horse Like a Horse: Optimize Your Horse's Nutrition for a Lifetime of Vibrant Health*. Indianapolis: Dog Ear Publishing, 2010.

Harris, Susan E. *The United States Pony Club Manual of Horsemanship: Basics for Beginners/D Level. 2nd ed.* Hoboken, NJ: John Wiley & Sons, 2012.

Henderson, Carolyn. *A Young Rider's Guide: Learn to Ride.* New York: Dorling Kindersley, 2005.

Lewis, Charni. *Braiding Manes and Tails: A Visual Guide to 30 Basic Braids.* North Adams, MA: Storey Publishing, 2008.

McFarland, Cynthia. *The Foaling Primer: A Month-by-Month Guide to Raising a Healthy Foal.* North Adams, MA: Storey Publishing, 2005.

Pence, Patricia. *Equine Dentistry: A Practical Guide.* Baltimore: Lippincott Williams & Wilkins, 2002.

Sellers, Mark, and Flossie Sellers. *Horse Health Matters: The Horse Owner's Guide to Equine Healthcare.* Morgan Hill, CA: EquiMed Press, 2015.

Thomas, Heather Smith. *Storey's Guide to Raising Horses.* North Adams, MA: Storey Publishing, 2010.

Watson, Valerie. *Manes and Tails.* Shrewsbury, UK: Quiller Publishing, 1986.

Index

P

Paddocks, 68, 71–73
Paint Horses, 17
Pants, 41
Pasturing, 68–69
Penning, 71–73
Percherons, 17
Peruvian Pasos, 18
Pests, 103–105
Play, 9
Polo, 116
Ponies, 5, 17, 19
Pony of the Americas, 26
Posting, 44
Preventive care, 97
Protein blocks, 63
Przewalski's horse, 27
Pulled manes, 84–85

Q

Quick-release knots, 54–55

R

Rain scald, 107
Reins, 37
Riding
　gaits, 43–45
　horse gear, 34–39
　human gear, 40–42
　safety, 52–53
Ringworm, 107
Roached manes, 85
Rocky Mountain Horses, 18
Rodeos, 116
Rolling, 109
Rope basics, 53–55
Routines, 120–123

S

Saddlebreds, 17
Saddles, 38
Safety, 47
　handling, 49–51
　riding, 52–53
　spaces, 48–49
Salt blocks, 62
Seed hay, 59
Senior citizens, 4
Sex, 31
Shedding blades, 81
Sheets, 93
Shelters, 69
Shetland Ponies, 19, 26
Shirts, 42
Showing, 113
Show jumping, 114
Shying, 53
Sires, 5
Size, 31
Sleep, 77
Soundness, 30
Space, and safety, 48–49, 52
Sponges, 81
Spooking, 53
Sports, 111–118
Spurs, 41
Stable cloths, 80
Stable flies, 104
Stabling, 75–76
　pastures, 68–70
　pens, 71–73
Stalling, 73–75
Stallions, 5, 7–8, 9
Standardbreds, 17, 23
Stirrups, 40
Stock horses, 18
Strangles, 108
Sweat scrapers, 82
Swedish Warmbloods, 18
Sweet itch, 108–109

T

Tack, 34–39
Teeth, 101–102
Temperament, 30

Acknowledgments

I am deeply indebted to my family, staff, horse community, and the professionals who checked this guide's facts and supported me through the writing of this book. Thank you to Dr. Hannah Mueller, DVM, at Cedarbrook Veterinary Care and Dr. Mary S. Delorey, DVM, at Northwest Equine Dentistry. I also want to thank the amazing editors at Callisto Media for their expertise, patience, and encouragement. For this I am grateful.

About the Author

Robyn Smith is a nurse living near Seattle with her husband, Mark, and her Yorkie, Grizzly. She owns and operates a riding school and teaches leadership and team-building skills to teens and adults. In her spare time, Robyn plays with a herd of adorable and much-loved horses, alpacas, and one llama.

For general information on our other products and services or to obtain technical support, please contact our Customer Care Department within the United States at (866) 744-2665, or outside the United States at (510) 253-0500.

Rockridge Press publishes its books in a variety of electronic and print formats. Some content that appears in print may not be available in electronic books, and vice versa.

Interior and Cover Designer: Stephanie Sumulong
Art Producer: Janice Ackerman
Editors: Kristen Depken and Eliza Kirby
Production Editor: Mia Moran

Cover and Interior Custom Illustration © 2019 Kate Francis

ISBN: Print 978-1-64611-345-3 | eBook 978-1-64611-346-0

R0